Give It To Your Guide:

How to Connect With and Accept Help From Spirit

by

Jezebel Jorge

with the invaluable assistance of Spirit Guide Odessa

*"When the student is ready
the teacher will appear."*
~ Buddah

Table of Contents

# Introduction

I am writing this book based on what I have learned in working with my spirit guides, especially my most powerful guide, Odessa. Being a practicing witch, my belief system may differ from yours, and that is perfectly okay. I believe each of us is entitled to walk our own unique spiritual path. I respect the beliefs of others and hope to have the same understanding shown in return.

The very intense bond I share with Odessa make us uniquely qualified to discuss the subject of Spirit Guides. I've never had a reading where her presence was not felt. In fact, at some gallery readings I have been asked to remove her from the circle because she tends to overpower the other spirits that are trying to come through.

Our goal in writing this book is to help others connect and attune with their Spirit Guides. I say our because Odessa is speaking to me as I type. This book could not be written without her guidance and support.

While I do consider myself to be a powerful medium, I am not the type who is capable of doing gallery readings. Odessa doesn't like me being exposed to that much energy. She is a very intense gatekeeper to the other side. No one comes through for me without her permission.

I've communicated with Spirit for most of my life. I can't remember a time when I felt no connection to the other side. I've seen full bodied spirits, heard them speak aloud, and almost always feel their presence.

One of my life's purposes is to tell Odessa's story and along the way learn from it as I enhance my own spiritual path. Her story will be released under the guise of fiction with a few name and detail changes to protect the not so innocent. You know, that whole legal liability thing, and out of respect for the ancestors of the people involved in her story.

But, enough about us, let's get down to the real purpose of this book...

## What are Spirit Guides?

Spirit Guides are the gatekeepers between the physical and spiritual realms. They bridge the gap between our lives here on Earth and that of those who have crossed over to the spiritual plane. Heaven, nirvana, summerland, the rainbow bridge for our pets, that place goes by many different names. For our purposes, I'll just refer to that spiritual plane as the other side.

Our guides are there for us to provide guidance, protection, and unwavering love. Their role is to assist and support us through our current life's journey.

We all have guides. Some of us are just more attuned to them than others. Anyone can learn to communicate with their guides. It's not a special gift. All you have to do is open your mind and your guides will gladly make their presence known.

There are various entitles on the spiritual realm. Ghosts, assorted angels, Gods and Goddesses, fairies or fey. We all connect to Spirit in our own personal ways. There is no right or wrong in connecting with Spirit. It's a matter of deciding what works best for you.

I don't claim to be an expert on angels. There are many books you can find to learn more about these beings. If you feel drawn to angels, I encourage you to do more research on that subject. Many mediums always invoke the four archangels before connecting with spirit. Me, I rely mainly upon Odessa. I know she's got my back and am extremely confidant in her power.

The one thing I do want to point out about angels is that unlike Spirit Guides, they have never been earthbound beings. They have never experienced life in human form. Maybe that is why I am more attached to my guides. They've been there and done that. They draw on their own past life experiences when helping us. You might prefer more divine guidance, and that is your choice, but I like knowing that Odessa has done this human thing a time or two.

Ghosts are also different from Spirit Guides. Just like in life, there are dark entities out there among the good or even the weak and harmless. My belief system has no place for the devil or hell. It irks me that some accuse witches of being devil worshipers when most of us don't even believe in the existence of such a being. It's kinda hard to worship something you don't believe exists.

I do however, respect both the powers of good and evil, darkness and light. I always wear a pentacle for protection and grounding. I would never being a session with Spirit without verbally stating that only those who walk in the light are allowed to make contact with me.

The media always seems to over-sensationalize evil or dark spirits. Most of those ghost hunting shows are a total scam. Any competent medium is going to be so closely bonded with their spirit guides that nothing is going to come through to them they can't handle. Maintaining the gateway to the other side is a guide's main responsibility. Maybe there are demons and evil spirits lurking out there, but I have never personally encountered anything of this nature. I've had a few incidents that made me uncomfortable and in that type of situation all I've had to do was tell Odessa to beef up her shield. If there is a spirit you don't want to make contact with politely tell them to go into the light and then just ignore them. They feed on your energy and fear is a most delicious food to them.

Remember, we often fear what we don't understand. Take the time to ask a presence why they are there or what they want from you. Maybe they are just lost and seeking attention. They can not and will not hurt you. That is a total load of crap propagated by the media.

We'll delve more into dealing with spirits in another book. For now, just know that your guide will NEVER let anything come through to you that you or they are not capable of handling.

Now on to the good stuff...

## Ascended or Master Guides

Your Master or Ascended Guide is the one guide who is with you from your birth until your death. Think of your Ascended Guide as your direct link to your higher power of choice.

You were first introduced to your Ascended Guide before your birth. This is when your guide helped you plan a path for this life's journey. You chose the life that you are living now based on your previous incarnations and what you hope to accomplish this time around. This guide assisted you in deciding when it was best for you to return to the physical realm. They helped you determine your sex, physicality, location, and even your parents.

This is also the guide who supervises and selects your other guides. When your guides need assistance this is who they turn to first. A Master Guide has completed their journey in the physical realm and has probably gone through several different assignments as a regular Spirit Guide. They are as close to an angel as you can get without direct intervention.

While you created your master plan before your birth, it's not as cut and dried as connecting the dots. You are given choices and options and the right to exercise your free will. Think of it like a role playing game. You choose an option and the other life choices fall into place based on each step of your journey.

Once your destiny has been determined, it has been said that the Master Guide will not step in and intervene or call in the assistance of angels until you've taken a serious discourse from your chosen path.

Your Master Guide will be the hardest guide to get to know for they are keen on practicing detachment. They are there when you need them, but only for serious matters. The little things are for your other guides to deal with.

You will most likely have no recent past life ties to your Master Guide. If that were the case they would be more inclined to get intimately involved in your current path. Your Master Guide will in some cases have past life connections to your other guides. Odessa shares a bond with my Master Guide, Iam.

Iam is a male presence. I picture him as blond and muscled. Strong and Solid. A Master Guide will allow you to see them in a way that best suits your needs. There is no right or wrong in your vision. Master Guides long ago gave up any attachments they may have had to their physical bodies.

I don't know Iam anywhere near as well as I know Odessa. I'm not supposed to know of him any more than what I need to sense his presence. He is there. I trust in him. I know he will send me the guides I need to complete this life's journey.

## Spirit Guides

Spirit Guides have three main purposes. Guidance, support and of course protection. Odessa is furiously protective of me, maybe to the point of being a little too extreme. If you are a medium you will find this to be both beneficial and sometimes a hindrance. She is what I refer to as my Alpha Guide. She is the gatekeeper in communicating with the other side. No one gets through without this guide's approval.

Any medium who claims they are communicating directly with the other side is not legit. It's your guides who act as the bridge. Messages come through Odessa and not from me. It's Spirit speaking and not the medium. Always remember that when considering a reading.

Shielding is one of the first things you learn after making a connection with your guide. They protect you by putting an energy field between you and anything they find unsafe or offensive. Think of it as a pure white light. If a situation is making you uncomfortable, picture this light and ask your guide to protect you. Trust me, this works.

Odessa swirls me in a powerful orange light as her favorite type of shield. I am able to call up this light whenever I need it. If I'm having a difficult day at work I spray a sage and citrus blend of essential oils and command Odessa to shield me from negative energy.

If you're having nightmares you can ask your guides to protect you as you sleep. I used to have a very terrifying reoccurring dream of a man hovering over my bed trying to rape me. Sometimes I would tell myself *this is just a dream, wake up*. I would then wake up in my dream thinking I wasn't dreaming and this time it was real. I stopped having this dream after connecting with my guides. I am almost convinced that instead of this being a dream it might have been a dark spirit that Odessa has since banished.

When I have nightmares now it is something Odessa allows to happen because I need to see this dream as a warning. I don't wake up scared, I know that she is protecting me and I was merely receiving a message.

Some people have very distinct guides for specific areas of their spiritual paths. These guides are labeled differently by different people and sometimes a guide is dormant to where you only sense them when you really need them. I'd like to discuss three specific types of guides in more detail.

Teacher Guides ~ These are guides with a very specific skill set and knowledge. I use this guide when I practice Reiki. This is the guide that works through my hands, it's not me. She was the Reiki Master. I am only a level two light worker. But, with her guidance, my hands will tingle and heat with her power.

If you are anxious about a test or an exam, this would be a good time to call in a this guide. Envision their presence while you study. Ask them to share their wisdom. Feel them watching over you as you take the test. Let them help you. Odessa does this for me in matters of public speaking. She likes the attention and comes shining through. I'm an extreme introvert who is glad to step back and let her bask in the spotlight.

Joy Guides ~ These are the guides who help you connect with your inner child. Their main purpose it to bring you happiness. This guide is usually a child or young adult. If you've ever seen a children connecting with their so-called imaginary friend, you might have witnessed this guide in action.

The Joy Guide is usually one of the easiest to connect with. Think back to your childhood and see if you can draw a name. The bond with these guides is very easy to indulge. They like to laugh and make you smile. Buy a balloon, flowers or candy. Your Joy Guide will react to these stimulants.

Joy Guides are usually attuned to their spirituality and are drawn to you by a common belief system. No, they're not nags about going to church or anything like that. They encourage you to embrace your higher power in the little things that make life fun. They're what makes you smile at silly stuff. Think puppies and kittens and birthday cake. Joy Guides are all about these type of things.

If you feel sad or depressed call upon your joy guide. Watch for them to send you little signs of love from the universe. Some people experience this by finding spare change. I keep a jar of coins I have picked up while out walking my dog. He once even found an old purse with several bills totaling over one hundred dollars and no form of identification. Look to your joy guide to bring you unexpected abundance.

Joy Guides love being asked for help. One of their favorite games is for you to ask them for little things such as a good parking spot in a crowded shopping center, a dry cart on a rainy day at the grocery store, your favorite song coming on the radio when you need to hear it. They take pleasure in spreading their joy.

Protection Guides ~ This guide is of a much more serious nature. These are usually very old and wise souls with many lifetimes of experience both in physical form and spiritual form as guides. Their primary responsibility is to keep you safe and secure. A lot of people have Native Americans as their Protection Guides. If you have a connection to the military your guide might be a soldier or maybe an old West gun slinger. This guide shows up in a form that you associate with protection and safety.

If you wake up scared in the middle of the night try summoning your Protection Guide. That is what he's there for. If you don't like driving in traffic try having a conversation with this guide. This guide has a lot to do with travel and transportation safety. He's the guy you speak with before getting on a boat or plane or setting off on a long road trip.

All of your guides enjoy being summoned. It's their job to help you and they delight in problem solving. Many times at night I'll ask Odessa a particular question and she will answer it in my dreams.

Spirit Guides are also excellent judges of character. If Odessa doesn't like some one I know they have no place in my life. She warned me about a particular person not exactly being on the level with their psychic abilities. I didn't want to believe her, but I later caught this person in various mistruths that Odessa sensed from the onset. When she tells me she doesn't like someone I now listen and heed her judgment. If she does like a person I try to go out of my way to make them a part of my life.

Guides can help you with finding things. Who hasn't occasionally misplaced their car keys. I lost a favorite Goddess pendant once. I used to wear it on a silver chain around my neck. I came in from walking my dog and realized it was gone. I panicked because this pendant has great sentimental value to me. It was getting late, but I still took a flashlight and tried to retrace the steps of our walk. I called upon Odessa and any other spirit who might offer assistance. The next morning I awoke to find the pendant on my nightstand. My guides had found it and returned the item to me.

If you are unsure about something ask your guides for a sign. I did this once with Odessa when I was struggling with a class on psychic development. I told her to show me a sign that my psychic abilities were real and not imagined. I then went outside to walk my dog and came across a snake under my balcony. Odessa adores snakes. A snake also symbolizes change. I took this as a sure sign of positive changes with my spiritual development.

Once you get to know your guides you will understand such subtle messages. The more you trust in your guides the more powerful they become. Then the more they can and are willing to do to help you.

Of course there are some things that guides just aren't capable of. Unless they had psychic gifts in their past incarnations your guides will have very limited psychic abilities. They can't predict the future. They can't give you winning lottery numbers. Your guides rely on their and your past life experiences to help you make decisions.

## Past Life Connections

Spirit Guides come into your life and stay as long as they are needed. They come to you assigned with specific goals and tasks to provide the help you need at particular times in your life. By helping you they are also completing their soul journey. There is much at stake for them as it is for you.

Your guide has most likely completed their physical journey. Odessa says they could choose to come back in human form. Not that she understands why a guide would wish to do so. Nevertheless, she says that option is there.

We most definitely have past life connections to our spirit guides. I know of three specific lives that Odessa and I shared. In our first life together that I remember we were lovers. Then we were sisters in blood and in the craft of witchery. In my previous life we shared a lover and I was a bit of a mentor to her, being about twenty years older and vastly more experienced.

The more time you spend with your guide and get to know them, the more you will learn about your previous incarnations. From what I have recalled of my previous life, I know why I selected to be born in a small town with a stable family. It was something my life lacked the last time around.

I also got my fear of bridges form dying in a car accident. Katie, me the last time around, crossed over after running her car into the Hudson River. If something scares you the way bridges terrify me, it most likely has a past life connection. If you've ever felt a strange connection to a city or place you probably spent time there in a previous life.

Katie lived most of her adult life in New York City. It is a place that both fascinates and scares me a little. Earlier in my life, when I was seeing a man who lived there, every time I would drive over the George Washington Bridge I always got a weird sense that I was coming home. It's the one bridge that never bothered me. I guess because of Katie's love for her life on the New York side of that bridge.

Your guides can distinctly sway your opinions of locations. Odessa has ties to Tampa, Florida. I know that is why I am drawn to Tampa. I see myself ending this life's journey in Tampa. Odessa has shown me this and helped me to understand some of my attractions and fears based on our past life experiences.

Your Master Guide selects the guides you work with based on bonds from past lives. Odessa, Carmella and Tabitha are all witches. It's what I am and what I relate to. It wouldn't have done me much good to get a devout and pious Bible thumper as a guide. Our beliefs would clash to where there would be nothing but frustration on both our parts.
This lifetime for me is a time of embracing my spirituality. That is why all my guides also so strongly represent my belief structure as a practicing witch. I hope my developing awareness of my past lives means I am getting close to completing my time in human form. We shall see, I suppose.

I think it might be easier to recall moments from past lives when there was not a lot of time between them. Katie crossed over in 1963 which didn't give me a lot of time to deal with that life before coming back again in 1967.

Those that suffer violent deaths always tend to come back quickly or hold off for a great number of years, giving their souls time to heal. I think a lot of murder victims ascend to guide status. Especially if they passed as children. They chose that life path for a reason and it was to learn to deal with those intense emotions to be better able to help others as guides.

Working with your guides is a great way to delve into your past lives. They provide the comfort and security you need to be ready to tackle tough issues. Their past life bond also makes it easier to pick up on shared memories. I've found past life regression meditations are an excellent way to get in touch with your inner selves.

Any good local New Age Shop should be able to help you find a spiritualist who does these meditations. Or if you are not comfortable in a group situation there are meditation CDs you can purchase to try in the comfort of your home. Listen to your guides and they will help you decide if you are ready to connect with your past and how to go about doing that.

**Meet My Guides**

Odessa is what I refer to as my Alpha Guide. She answers only to Iam, and of course to me. There are other guides, but for me they only play minor roles in my life. Odessa is a control freak and has a hard time delegating authority. She takes her alpha role very seriously. In fact, I think she'd tell Iam to back off and take a powder if she thought she could get away with it. We are slowly learning to trust in the other guides and give them a little more leeway.

My Teacher Guide ~ Carmella

This is the guide who comes through and takes control when I practice Reiki. Carmella was a Reiki Master in several of her past incarnations and has taken that gift with her to the spiritual realm.

This is the guide Odessa trusts the most because they have shared several lifetimes together and were best friends in their last earthbound incarnation. Carmella was an emergency room nurse, and later when she got tired of dealing with hospital politics, she became a mid-wife and holistic healer. She's a pleasantly plump woman of Haitian decent. Her skin is as black as Odessa's is pale and she has cornrows that jingle when she's excited. Carmella is also a witch. She, more than any of the other guides, looks out for my health.

My Joy Guide~ Tabitha

Tabitha is responsible for all things happiness. She's a teenager who has never lived a human existence past her teens. A lot of Joy Guides are eternal kids. I see Tabitha as a petite redhead. In many of her human incarnations she was a powerful psychic and medium. If you've read any of my Ring Dreams fictional series, little red haired Tabitha Dalton, the most powerful DeFliehr witch ever, strongly resembles my Tabitha.

My Protection Guide ~ Alex

Alex, came to life for me as a character in my Ring Dreams series of novels. Yeah, he's that Alex. His father's parents were Russian immigrants. His maternal grandmother was a Chinese mail order bride purchased by a Southerner with more money than sense. I see Alex as self-sufficient, a tall and tough, badass of a dude. He guards me by intimidation and pure brute force.

Odessa

Before we move on to meeting your guides I'd like to give you some background on how I met Odessa. Feel free to skip this section if you're not interested. I promise she won't feel slighted and want to put snakes in your bed. We're including this because we didn't meet in typical Spirit Guide fashion. I met Iam through a guided meditation, the way that usually happens in most first communication with your guides. Alex and Tabitha revealed themselves to me over time, after I'd developed a gift of communicating with spirit, but Odessa...

While working on my first novel I attended a writer's workshop in Raleigh, North Carolina. It was there, walking my dog through a cemetery, that I by chance stumbled upon Odessa's grave. The instant I read her headstone I knew Odessa was perfect name for the ghostly grandmother in *Hexed*. Little did I know that the real Odessa would follow me home.

I think she's been with me since soon after her death in 1985. I just never realized it until our bond strengthened when I came across her grave a few years ago. She officially revealed herself to me as my guide about a year later.

To make things all the more interesting, Odessa decided to come to me on my birthday. I'd taken the day off from work because I never work on my birthday and I was preparing to move to a bigger apartment later that week. My boy toy came over that morning and the sex with him raised my energy vibration. Then I ate some chocolate. That, on top of the sex, along with a couple bottles of Smirnoff Ice, had my energy vibration zooming to where I couldn't really focus on packing. I decided to take a nap.

I was just drifting off to sleep when Odessa came to me in full bodied human form. She stood over my bed and introduced herself and explained that she was much more than a name on a headstone, or a character in my story, she is my guide and through me she is going to tell her story.

"I am real. I am real," she continually repeated. I can still hear those words ringing in my ears.

While seeing any full bodied spirit is totally amazing, Odessa took things to a whole other level because she is a stunningly beautiful woman. She has long naturally red hair that streams to her ass in elaborate curls. She is tall and waifish, very slender and fine boned. She has big piercing green eyes, pouty lips and flawless alabaster skin. She is at once intimidating, yet very fragile with her delicate features and absolutely exquisite beauty.

A lot of guides never reveal themselves physically with such stunning clarity. I think she clings to her human form because of how beautiful she was in her previous human incarnations. She's the type of woman who turns every head when she walks into a room.

Odessa spent most of that first day telling me her story. She told me she had once walked among the living and that we had a mutual acquaintance. I later contacted this person and he verified her identity. Since then I have talked to a few more people who knew her. One person, who she later introduced me to, knew her very well as she was the mistress of one of his closest friends.

Her visit left me so drained that I fell into sleep so deep I didn't hear the phone when my boy toy tried to reach me to come back over that evening. I finally awoke the next morning with extreme chills and felt so weak that I found it hard to get out of bed. My head was swimming and my whole body ached. It was all I could do to call in sick to work and go to see a doctor.

My temperature and blood pressure always run low, but this time they were lower than normal. Instead of running a fever, the nurse had to check my temperature three time to convince herself I wasn't dead. They did a flu swab that came up negative. I'm prone to inner ear infections, so that was checked with the same result.

The doctor was basically baffled. She could tell I wasn't faking. Not sure what to do for me, she told me to drink lots of fluids and get some rest. I got the doctor's excuse I needed to take off the rest of the week and went home to bed. The next two days are a blur. I don't remember finishing my packing or much of any of the moving process other than waking up in my new apartment. I guess Odessa and the boy toy did all the work. I couldn't really tell you, because I have no idea how I got settled in the new place.

After the move I went about contacting the people Odessa wanted me to speak with to confirm the events of her previous life. Every single thing she has told me has since been verified. Some of the connections still amaze me. We share a strong link with that one particular man we both know. He was my first love, Odessa is not quite as fond of him. I've become the best of friends with the other man she introduced me to.

I constantly surprise him with things I can tell him that I really shouldn't have any way of knowing. Well, other than through Odessa. I told him what her Beloved's office looked like down to the funky ugly couch in the corner. I described her house in detail before we drove by it the first time I went to visit him in Tampa. Odessa was upset because it had been a salmon color when she lived there and now it's a rather garish shade of yellow.

Every time Odessa tells me something I try my best to confirm it. Google is an amazing research tool. I think she gets a kick out of my fact checking and takes great satisfaction with each, *"I told you so."*

Okay, enough about Dess, lets get down to the business of meeting your guides.

## How Do Guides Communicate?

By now you are probably wondering how I get messages from my guides. Or more importantly, how you can communicate with your guides. Odessa and I share a very intense bond to the point where she's inside my head a lot more than she probably needs to be.

When you first make contact with your guide it might be nothing more than a sensation. A word or specific images popping into your head. In the beginning this will most likely occur through meditation and especially dreams. After you get to a point you just feel your guides presence and communicating with them is just like talking to an actually person. That's the way it is with me and Odessa. We carry on conversations inside my head.

This telepathy is the most common way of communicating with your guide. When you get to a certain point you just know it's them speaking to you. I'm sure at sometime everyone has acknowledged that little voice inside their head. That voice is most likely your guide trying to get your attention. This is often referred to has hearing with your inner ear.

If you do hear your guide speak aloud it's something important, possibly life threatening. This rarely happens, but when or if it does it is something you never forget.

Communication can also be sensory based. The temperature used to drop when Odessa would appear. I would get chills. Thankfully she's stopped doing the deep freezes since I know her presence without the icy blasts. Sometimes a guide will turn a light, television or radio on or off, or move things around. You might smell something. I have a spirit that visits us who emits a very intoxicating fragrance. I always smell him before I sense his presence.

Some guides will show you images of something of significance. This might be a vision or an actual thing, such as the snake Odessa sent to me. Birds are commonly used in this way. There are no set specifics, just something that resonates with you. At first you might start out getting flashes that will eventually develop into full length movies played out inside your head.

You will often just feel a calming presence when your guide comes to you. When Odessa is especially emotional I sometimes see red and silver swirls of energy. Orbs are very common indication of paranormal activity. Sometimes you'll see a shadow of a fleeting movement out of the corner of your eye.

There have been a few occasions when I have seen Odessa in full physical form just as if she were a living breathing person. It's rare to see a fully solidified spirit of any sort so be sure to appreciate the occurrence and honor your guide appropriately.

## Preparing to Meet Your Guides

The way I met Odessa is far from typical. If that has happened to you, I guess you aren't reading this for any reason other than curiosity. If your guide hasn't yet knocked you upside the head with a show stopping introduction, there are tools that you can use to make their acquaintance. The most important thing to have is an open mind. I'm assuming that is already a given, since I doubt you'd be reading this otherwise.

The next step is to gather a few tools for this journey. You may already have these things at your disposal. If not, a shopping trip is in order.

Recommended Items:

Sacred Object ~ For me, this is my pentacle pendant. I never work with Spirit without a pentacle. Actually, I wear a pentacle on a silver chain pretty much 24/7.
A pentacle is a Pagan symbol of protection. It's a star inside a circle. The five points of the star symbolize the four elements. Water, Fire, Earth, Air and most importantly their link to Spirit.

My pendant is silver and centered with a small black circular stone. I felt the pull of this particular piece while browsing in my favorite store and just knew it was the one for me.

Your Sacred Object is a deeply personal choice. It can be anything you choose that makes you feel secure and protected. If you are Christian, it might be a cross. It could even be your wedding band, a favorite pair of earrings, or just something you like to wear or hold that gives you a sense of peace.

Sage Incense ~ This is used for cleansing your workspace. It's always a good idea to burn sage when working with Spirit. It will release any negative energy and supposedly keeps away dark or evil entities.

Candle ~ I recommend a white candle to symbolize purity of intentions. This is totally your call on which candle you find appealing and are drawn to. Different colors do have different connotations when working candle magick. An entire book can be written on this subject and many have with much more in depth information. Here is a very basic break down of color choices:

White ~ Purity of intentions
Red ~ Passion and sexual energy
Pink ~ Love and friendship
Yellow ~ Positive energy
Orange ~ Creativity
Green ~ Abundance
Purple ~ Healing
Blue ~ Connection to Spirit
Black ~ Rids negativity
Brown ~ Grounding
Gold ~ God or Goddess
Silver ~ Angelic presence

There are Reiki charged or spell candles that you can purchase, but a plain candle from the Dollar Store will work just as well. A candle is just a prop to help harness your intention and focus. Don't get me wrong, candle magick is very powerful and one of my favorite tools, but really, a candle by itself is just a candle. If you are a practicing witch feel free to add your own candle magick to this journey. Otherwise, just find a candle you like.

Notebook and writing utensil ~ A plain notebook works just fine. Once again the Dollar Store might be your friend. It helps to have something handy to write down anything that comes to you. You might think you'll remember something later, but it's best to put it in writing just in case you become overwhelmed.

Now let's go shopping...

If there is a New Age shop in your area it would be a great idea to pay them a visit. Take your time and browse the store. Pay special attention to anything that you seem especially drawn to. Your guide might already be at work, showing you things that appeal to them.

If you are not able to go to a store, shopping online works just as well.

## Meeting Your Guides

This is best done on an evening when you have plenty of time and privacy. You may also find there to be more energy on the night of a full moon. The important thing is to be in a place where you are relaxed and comfortable. If you are in a hotel room be sure to sage before getting started. Even if you are at home in the comfort of your own bedroom you can leave the sage burning by a window or the door.

It's okay to pour a glass of wine or mix a drink. One drink is fine if it will help you to relax. Just don't over indulge. It's also good to have a light snack. A piece of chocolate is good. Sugar will raise your energy vibration.

If you like incense, go ahead and light up one of your favorite scents. Odessa is quite fond of lotus. Light a candle. I recommend blue for connecting with spirit.

Now it's time for a cleansing bath. This will allow you to unwind, ease your nerves and relax. I am a Pisces, so I am intensely drawn to water. I do my best candle magick while soaking in my tub. Take as long as you like to enjoy your bath Your goal is to leave all your tension and stress in the bathwater. Send your worries down the drain.

When you are ready, you can change into something comfortable or remain naked. That part is entirely up to you. Find a spot where you can relax without any distractions. Background music is fine as long as you don't get distracted by the words. No TV or radio. This is your quiet time.

Be sure to bring along a bottle of water because communicating with spirit can be dehydrating. Sipping on water will help your thought process.

Go ahead and light your white candle and get comfortable. You can lie down or sit in a comfy chair. It is important to not cross your arms or legs as that can block your energy vibration. This is the time to state aloud that only those who walk in the light are allowed to make contact with you. Also, verbally welcome your guides. A simple, "Hello, I am open to receive your messages and I am eager to meet you, my guide," will work just fine.

Voice your intentions as you see fit.

Close your eyes and take several deep cleansing breaths. With each exhale release any negative thoughts or energies. Every inhale replaces the bad with good loving and positive emotions.

When your heart rate begins to slow, imagine your body enveloped in a pure and radiant white light. If you are drawn to another color, as Odessa and I prefer orange, swirl that color amid the white light. Float in the light. Allow the light to lift you up and carry your spirit outside your body.

You are about to embark on a life changing journey. A trip so exciting that you can't feel your footsteps on a set of golden stairs. Take your time walking up these stairs. Breath in all your favorite scents, soothing lavender, coffee brewing, cookies baking, whatever you associate with happiness. Listen to all your favorite sounds, laughter, birds chirping, a babbling brook. Appreciate all the wonders that surround you.

When you reach the top of the stairs you will find four open doors. At your own pace stand in each doorway and decide which scene you find the most appealing. This is your journey and everything is your choice.

The first doorway leads to a wooded trail laden with lush moss that leads to a garden. The grass is between your feet is soft and think and so very green. The soil is fertile.

There are plants of every imaginable variety and their scent is intoxicating. You look up at the sky and see a bird fly by and land on a tree limb. The bird warbles a song just for you. The sun caresses your skin as you sit down in the grass. You are one with the earth.

The second doorway opens to a candlelit wood paneled cabin. There are several down pillows in front of a roaring fire. You can smell hot cocoa and buttery popcorn. You take a seat amid the pillows and snuggle with a blanket as you watch the dancing flames. The heat of the fire feels so good against your skin, enveloping you in a perfect warmth. You are one with the fire.

The third doorway reveals a balcony overlooking a snowy cliff. You lean over the edge and feel the wind brushing your skin like a lover's embrace. There is a storm brewing in the distance. Lightening flashes across the sky. The air is heavy with the scent of rain. The wind is whipping, but you're safe. There is a swing on the balcony. You can take a seat on the swing and move with the wind, safe and protected on your high mountain perch. You are one with the air.

The final doorway leads you to a beach. The water is so blue and melts into the horizon. The weather is perfect. You can feel the sand between your toes, taste the salt water breeze on your tongue. That water is calling your name, luring you to step into it, and just float away. You are one with the water.

It's time to make your choice and go through the doorway that screams to your heart. This is where you belong. This is where you are at peace. This is where your soul sings.

Take a few minutes to get comfortable in your sacred spot. Sink into the green grass. Feel the heat of the fireplace. Let the wind whip through your hair. Float peacefully the warm water. You are free. You are at peace. You are at one with your destiny.

When you are ready call out to your guides, use your own words. Let them know you are here. You are ready to greet them with open arms. You want to receive their love, guidance and wisdom.

*I am here. I am ready. Hello, my guides. Please come to me. Reveal yourself to me. I want to know you. I want to feel your love. You understand me like no other. I want to know you. I want you to know me. My heart is open. Come to me. Share my thoughts and dreams. Make me laugh with your humor. Guide me with your divine wisdom. I am here. I am ready to meet you.*

Feel your guide take your hand. Look up and acknowledge their presence.

*Hello, dear guide.*

This is your time to connect. Your guide is only going to reveal what you are ready to know. You may see flashes of color. Maybe an animal. There might not be anything for you to see physically. Perhaps your guide is so old that they have no memory of their earthbound form. Just because you can't see something, does not mean it is not there. You guide doesn't care how you see them. Dress them up, make them laugh. As long as you do it lovingly, they won't care.

Ask your guide their name. Ask their story. Ask of your past connections.

This is your special time. The time between you and your guide. Just the two of you. No one has to know what is said or shown. Just relax, listen, absorb.

Take as long as you like. You have all night. Your guide is delighted to be acknowledged. They are so happy that you have reached out to them. Your guide is smiling up at you. Their smile radiates the purest, deepest love that you could ever imagine.

This is your time.

When you are ready, thank your guide for coming to you. Exchange your goodbyes for now. Know that you can come here any time you choose. You can now summon your guide anytime you need them. They are always there. They are always with you.

Let's go back down the stairs. Come back to your physical body. Take a moment to wiggle your fingers and toes. Breathe in and out. You are home.

Now take some time to write down your thoughts. Drink your water. Savor the moment. This is your time. If you like, you can continue the process by asking your guide to come visit you in your dreams.

The more you practice the communion with your guides, the deeper you will bond. Your relationship will grow with each visit. Set aside at least one night a week to spend some time with your guide, just the two of you getting to know each other. Make visiting with your guide a routine ritual. They are always there for you. This relationship works on your terms.

There is no right or wrong.

## Tools for Strengthening The Spirit Bond

Tarot Cards ~ There are an array of Tarot cards to suit any specific taste. If you are just starting out, listen to your instincts. It would probably be a good idea to select a deck with a through guidebook with different layouts and card descriptions and interpretations. Tarot is not one of my specialties, so I won't attempt to offer advice on their use.

Spirit Boards ~ I love spirit boards. I have a custom board with a pentacle and snakes. Odessa adores snakes so this board really resonates for her. I know there is a lot of negativity about the use of Ouija boards and I think most of it is a load of crap. I know Odessa is a strong enough gatekeeper to keep me safe from any dark entities. I am also confident enough in my channeling abilities to quickly stop any unwanted spiritual encounters.

If the board makes you nervous or uncomfortable, by all means stay away from them. If you find them interesting, then don't be afraid to give them a try. Any board will work. In a pinch I've used one from the Target toy department. To increase the board's energy write your name on it or draw some symbols. I doodled a pentacle and wrote Odessa's name on the one I used.

Before working with the board, it is important to state your intention of only invoking spirits who walk in the light. I personally cast a circle and state that no one gets through without Odessa's permission.

I've only had one uncomfortable experience with a spirit board and it was my mindset and not the spirit who made me uneasy. I was using the board on a Samhain Eve when the veil was at it's thinnest and channeled a man who murdered one of my closest friends. He was her husband and I knew him and all the details and circumstance of the murder / suicide. He gave me his initials and I instantly knew who he was. I refused to say his name to weaken his power and asked him to leave. I got up from the table, turned on the lights and immediately saged the motel room.

Looking back, I can see that I totally overreacted. I wish I'd given him the opportunity to communicate with me. If he ever chooses to come through to me again I will be open to hearing from him. Just not that close to Samhain and not in a strange place.

Automatic Writing ~ Odessa and I do this daily. Open a new document on your computer and invite your guide to come in and speak. A notebook works just as well. It's a similar process to the meditation. Center yourself. Invite your guide and let them have at it.

Type a question. Meditate on it. Let your guide speak through your hands.

You'll be surprised what you might find at the end of a writing session. I honestly have no memory of some of the things Odessa types through me until I go back and reread them.

Guided Meditation CDs or workshops ~ There are many great options available. You can find these on Amazon or internet search engines. Any good New Age store will have a selection and most likely someone there to direct you to the best CDs or recommend classes.

This is one of those go with your gut feeling selections. If you are drawn to a particular CD, your Guide is probably pushing you in that direction. If you are short on cash, you might try checking your local library to see what choices are available.

Dream Work ~ This might be the easiest method for a beginner. Every night before you fall asleep state your intentions to meet with your guide. Invite your guide to join you in your dreams.

It also helps to drink a glass of water right before falling asleep. Don't forget to keep your journal or a handheld recorder by your bed to record your dreams. I know you think you'll remember, but record everything just to be safe.

Gallery Readings ~ If you find a gallery reading in your area you might want to check it out. Before going in, state your intentions. Think about meeting your guide while the medium is doing the readings. Thinking about a spirit always makes the stronger.

Don't be disappointed if you don't get a message this way. I know Odessa shields me at most gallery readings to where I don't get any type of message. If I know the reader they sometimes come to me afterwards and tell me Odessa was throwing up a shield to where they couldn't get anything for me. Not getting any message at all can also mean your guide is not comfortable with the reader.

If your guide is over-protective, gallery readings won't work for you. Then again, if your guide likes the reader, they might make themselves known. My friend Teresa met Odessa this way. If your guide doesn't like the reader she can wreck havoc on a reading by messing with the reader's energy. Odessa has done this to the point where I have had to remove myself from the energy field.

Always trust your guide over anyone else. Your guides know you best and are always protecting you.

Readings From A Medium ~ A one on one session with a medium might work a little better than a gallery reading, at least to validate what you think you already know.

The same disclaimer holds double for this one. If your guide doesn't like the person doing the reading you won't get anything. Or even worse, your guide might decide to have a little fun with the medium and send them a bunch of made up stuff that will come through in your reading.

## Tips for Increasing Your Connection With Spirit

Trust ~ This is the absolute first thing that has to be established. Trust comes from getting to know your guide on a most intimate level. The more you trust your guide, the more they will do for you.

Practice ~ Engage your guide as often as possible. The longer you work together and the better you know each other, the greater your combined powers.

Privacy ~ The more time you can spend alone with your guide, the better you will understand them. I live alone. Most of the time it's just me, my dog and Odessa. I feel her with me all the time. When I do go visit my family or have friends visit I don't sense her presence as strongly. I can still summon her, but unless it's the friend she has the bond with, it's like a mini-break in our connection.

Diet ~ A clean diet will greatly approve your channeling abilities. I have Celiac Disease and since I've stopped eating gluten I have had a dramatic increase in my powers. Some mediums go as far as to become total Vegans. Odessa would eat dairy products after properly thanking the cow, but she never consumed any meat. If it once had a soul, she didn't eat it.

Water ~ Hydration is vital to keeping up your energy vibration. If your thoughts start to feel muddled, try upping your water intake. You will feel a difference.

Fasting ~ Not consuming any solid food for a 24-48 hour period will have a direct impact on your communication with spirit. Just be sure to drink plenty of water while doing this. It's okay to skip on the food, but when you do this, you need to up your water intake.

Medications ~ Don't stop taking any medications without talking to your doctor, but there are a lot of medications, especially anti-depressants, that will interfere with your ability to communicate with spirit. Odessa was incessant about getting me off Thyroid medication. She was right, the medication had messed with my system. After I stopped taking the pills I slept better and was much more clear headed.

Reiki Attunement ~ This is a Japanese technique for stress reduction and relaxation that promotes healing by aligning the body's chakras.
This one is a biggie. If your chakra's are out of balance, you're going to have problems in all facets of your life. My powers soared after getting my Reiki attunements.

Working with light and balance is so important that we'll continue this subject in following chapter.

# Reiki and Light Work

Reiki is based on the idea that life force energy flows through us and is what causes us to be alive. If your energy is low, you are more likely to get sick or feel stress. When your energy vibration is high, you will be healthy and happy.

Communicating with Spirit is greatly enhanced with a high energy vibration. If you've ever been to a gallery reading you've probably felt the temperature rise when all the spirits converge. My hands are tingling as I type this, just from thinking about raising my vibration. Your mind is your most powerful tool in exploring new plans of spirituality.

Reiki is the combination of two Japanese words:
Rei ~ God's Wisdom or The Higher Power.
Ki ~ Life Force Energy.

Reiki is spiritually guided life force energy.

Reiki is used to balance human energy fields or auras and energy centers called chakras to allow the body to function at it's highest frequency.

The aura is the electromagnetic field that surrounds every human, organism, and object in the universe. We've already mentioned the power of the white light that leads the way to the other side. Once you learn to work with your guides you will experience how to manipulate these energy fields.

There are seven auric fields:

Physical ~ Physical sensations. What you can see, feel, taste, touch and smell.

Etheric ~ Emotions of the self. Self acceptance and love.

Vital ~ The rational mind.

Astral ~ Emotional relations with others. Human interactions.

Lower Mental ~ Divine will within.

Higher Mental ~ Divine love.

Spiritual ~ Divine mind.

We're covering this topic because your spirit guides will be able to read your auras. When they show you a particular color you want to have some understanding of what they might be referring to. An aura can be thought of as a map of thoughts and feelings surrounding a person. Aura reading can be very helpful in holistic healing. If you want to continue to learn to channel other spirits this is important because your guide may show you these colors to help you receive messages. Remember that all legit channeling is done through spirit guides. No human has a direct link to the other side without the help of their guides.

Here is a very basic breakdown on understanding aura colors:

Red ~ Relates to the physical body, heart or circulation. A deep red is an indication of grounding, strong will, active. A muddied red indicates anger. A clear red is of a sexual or competitive nature. A pinkish red signifies love and romance.

Orange ~ Relates to reproductive organs and emotions. This color indicated sexual energy, creativity, power, and excitement. Odessa uses this color with me a lot to spur my creativity.

Yellow ~ Related to the spleen and life energy. This is a sign of an awakening, inspiration, or a playful and easy going energy. A light pale yellow is a sign of psychic or spiritual energy. Lemon yellow shows a fear of losing control. Gold is of a spiritual nature. A murky yellow indicates stress or fatigue.

Green ~ Relates to heart and lungs. This color indicates growth and balance. A bright emerald green is a sign of a healer. A yellowish green is a creative communicator. A dark green indicates jealousy or resentment.

Turquoise ~ Relates to the immune system. This indicates sensitivity and compassion.

Blue ~ Relates to the throat and thyroid. Think calm, cool and collected when seeing a lot of blues. A soft blue indicates peace and clarity. A royal blue is a sign of clairvoyance and generosity. A dark blue indicates a fear of failure or that someone is hiding something.

Indigo ~ Relates to the third eye and indicates deep feelings.

Violet ~ Relates to the crown and nervous system.

Lavender ~ Indicates imagination and vision.

Silver ~ A sign of abundance, both material and spiritual. In metallic form it indicates receptiveness. In a gray form it is often a sign of illness or health concerns.

Gold ~ A sign of enlightenment and divine protections. Think angels and the highest good.

Black ~ This color captures light and consumes it. It's not always negative as it is sometimes an indication of transformation. Giving up the old in favor of a new outlook or path. Black is also indication of lingering emotional pain from a previous life.

White ~ This color is a reflection of other energy. It indicates purity, existence on a higher plane. Angelic qualities. If you see white sparkles it is an indication of angels in your midst. Seeing white around a woman is also a sign of a possible welcomed pregnancy.

Earth Colors ~ This shows grounding.

Rainbow ~ This is the color or a Reiki Master or powerful light worker.

Pastels ~ Indicate heightened sensitivity.


Chakras are the points where auras enter and release from the body. Chakras in Sanscrit translates to wheel or disk. There are seven main chakras and the goal of Reiki is to keep them aligned and balanced.

Once you learn your chakras it's a good idea to include them in every meditation. I usually go through and envision cleansing and opening my chakras before going to the heart of the meditation. This is done by imagining that color pulsing and radiating from that point of the body.

Root Chakra ~ Located at the base of the spine. This is red and is used for grounding.

Sacral Chakra ~ Located in the lower abdomen. This is orange and focuses on sexuality and creativity.

Solar Plexus Chakra ~ Located below the diaphragm. This is yellow and deals with self-worth and confidence.

Heart Chakra ~ Located on the chest. This is green and deals with matters of the heart. How you relate to others.

Throat Chakra ~ Located in the throat. This is blue and focuses on communication. If you are having trouble putting your thoughts into words, this is the chakra that would need balancing.

Third Eye Chakra ~ Located in the center of the forehead. This is Indigo and indicates self-awareness.

Crown Chakra ~ Located at the top of the head. This is white or sometimes lavender. This is the connection to spirit and the divine.

If you are ever given the opportunity to do so, I would encourage anyone to participate in a Reiki Circle. It's really hard to describe the energy vibration unless it is something you have experienced. Once your vibration is heightened your hands will heat up and tingle with power. The energy vibration will make the temperature of the room increase. It's important to have water handy because it can be dehydrating. Animals are drawn to the energy. I've seen cats hop up on the table and dogs crash underneath it.

In one circle I had the pleasure of being at the Crown Chakra of a powerful medium and psychic and the merging of our combined energies was a total high. Let's just say you usually sleep very well after a Circle.

Reiki isn't of itself a sexual experience, but if you are already intimate with a partner it can produce some sparks. I've found it extra hard to shield from a lover after a Reiki session.

Which brings us to the importance of shielding. If you aren't careful with asking your guide for shielding you can pick up the energy of others. Sometimes it's a really nice thing, like when I was doing the Crown Chakra above. This is especially true if you are an empath, which I am with certain people.

An empath is able to feel another person's emotions as if they were their own. Great for joy and happiness, not so good when picking up physical pain. I have a very strong bond with someone to where when his ankle hurts I feel the same pain. Despite being in different time zones, I still know when I need to call and tell him to take a pain killer. I also feel the relief of the medication.

But, back to shielding, when doing Reiki you always want to shield to keep from picking up other people's energy. The best way is to have your guide use a mirror between you and the other people.

If you would like to learn more about Reiki I recommend reading, *Essential Reiki: A Complete Guide to an Ancient Healing Art* by Diane Stein. This book is a great resource and used by a lot of Reiki instructors when teaching classes.

## Closing Thoughts

Your relationship with your Spirit Guides is a deeply personal experience and unique to every individual. I hope I've given you some insight on the subject and helped you make contact with your guides.

Communicating with Spirit is an ongoing process and just like with any skill it requires practice. Don't give up if you don't instantly make contact or if your messages seem vague. It takes time and patience.

If you have any questions or comments I can be reached via email at jezebeljorge@gmail.com

Good luck on your journey and Blessed Be...

*Jezebel & Odessa*

## About The Author

Jezebel Jorge is a practicing witch and gifted medium. When she's writing it usually feels like she's merely taking dictation for the voices running amok inside her head.

She currently lives in Nashville, TN with a spoiled rotten Golden Retriever / Great Pyrenees mix named Harry Potter and a mouthy spirit guide with a fondness for snakes who just happens to be named Odessa.

To find out more about Jezebel Jorge, please visit:
www.witchlitchick.com
www.jezebeljorge.com.

## Other Books by Jezebel Jorge

Ring Dreams Novels:
Wicked Desires
Wanton
Dirty Weekend
Hexed
Desire
Vexed
The Courtney Collection

Shattered (A Ring Dreams YA)

Infinity - An Anti-Valentine's Day Novella

Odessa's Stories:
Under My Skin
The Lady Is A Tramp
Fly Away
Always
Illicit

Non-Fiction:
Everything You Ever Wanted to Know About Spirit
Boards But Were Afraid To Ask